CHELMSFORD CATHEDRAL

Christus Rex by Peter Ball.

THE DEAN'S WELCOME

Welcome to Chelmsford Cathedral. Chelmsford Cathedral is no vast, vaulted hall. Its qualities are more jewel-like: small, light, colourful, precious and cherished. When you walk in the building it seems to welcome you. It lifts the spirit and its silence sings.

Since September 2000 the Cathedral has been crowned by Peter Eugene Ball's magnificent sculpture of *Christ in Glory*. The outstretched arms reinforce the welcome, and the soaring figure inspires faith.

Although we receive many visitors, we are not tourist led. When you walk in you usually find people at prayer. The candlestand never goes out. Although we are a busy Cathedral, being a popular venue for concerts, lectures, civic events, school prize-giving and university graduation ceremonies, the heart of the Cathedral is the daily rhythm of worship with beautifully sung choral services. Despite all the busyness, the Cathedral is an easy place to pray in. God is here in this holy place in its stillness and in its bustle.

This Cathedral has been a parish church for centuries and remains so. It became a

Cathedral in 1914 and the Bishop's throne, 'Cathedra', prominently placed under the East Window, testifies to that. The Diocese of Chelmsford is now the second largest diocese in the country.

You may also wish to know about St. Cedd's Chapel at Bradwell-on-Sea. In 653 AD St. Cedd landed at Bradwell-on-Sea to bring Christianity to the East Saxons. He built his church at Bradwell and it is still there to this day and well worth a visit. We are heirs of his work.

I hope you enjoy your visit to this jewel of a Cathedral.

The Town

In the year of the Norman Conquest a small rural manor with a population of five villeins and their households was held by Bishop William of London. Bounded on the east by the river Chelmer, and on the south by the river Can or 'Great River', it stood on land which rose gently between the two converging river valleys to a broad expanse of higher ground. Bishop William was a Norman and the manor remained in his hands and those of his successors, the powerful bishops of London, for 500 years. On these facts hangs the story of the founding of the parish of Chelmsford and the building of this church. Four centuries earlier St Cedd had fulfilled a mission among the East Saxons during which he built 'minsters' including St. Peter's-on-the-Wall which still survives at Bradwell-on-Sea (please see page 22). He was consecrated bishop and, according to the Venerable Bede, 'established communities of the servants of Christ and taught them to maintain the discipline of the regular life so far as these untutored folk were then capable of doing'. The Chelmer and the Can and the marshy ground at their confluence were, however, formidable obstacles to travel, a Saxon invader called Ceolmaer having given his name to a notorious fording place. It is therefore not surprising that in the 11th century the Bishop's manor was of no importance. In the early 12th century, however, by the initiative of the lord of the manor, the same Bishop Maurice who began the rebuilding of St. Paul's Cathedral in 1087, the 'Great River' was bridged. With this bridge and the ford over the Chelmer on the highway between London and Colchester, conditions were right for the creation of a town. Another bishop, William of Ste Mère-Eglise, founded it here at 'Ceolmaer's ford' in the centre of the shire, at a crossing place with a steady flow of traffic. He acquired grants from King John between 1199 and 1201 for a weekly market in what is now the high street, an annual fair and the settlement of the town with freeholders.

Chelmsford High Street in 1762; showing the church in the background, and the judge's procession to the Tudor assize court building and the watercourse (Ceolmaer's ford), which had flowed through the town since the 14th century. Painting by David Ogborne.

The Church

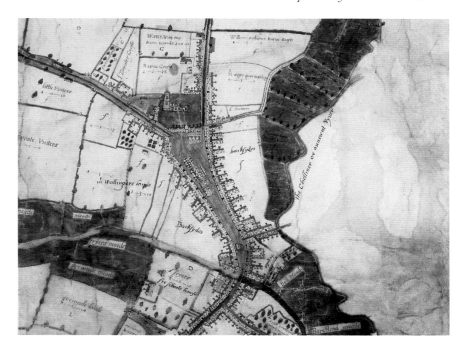

This early map clearly shows the Cathedral standing in its grounds, immediately north of the Market Place.

One of the energetic 12th century bishops of London (it is not known which), began the building of a Norman church dedicated to st. Mary serving the two manors of Chelmsford, and Moulsham south of the Great River. The first authenticated incumbent, Richard de Gorges, was presented in 1242, the living remaining in the gift of the bishops of London until the 16th century. By the 15th century, the church was regarded as too unassuming in appearance for a county town and too small for the diocesan business conducted in it, so in the latter half of that century and the early 16th century it was rebuilt. From this rebuilding the cathedral church evolved through 500 years. Alongside progress there were setbacks. In the mid-16th century the church plate was sold to pay for repairs; draughts, rain, starlings and storm damage are all cited. But in 1591 the church was described as '*goodlye, seemely, and large … with manie goodlye pues, one goodlye steeple ymbattled … and foure belles*'. It suffered damage in the disorders before and during the Civil War largely through compliance with Parliament's ordinances against superstition and idolatry. In 1641, £5 was paid to remove the pictures of the Blessed Virgin Mary and Christ from the great east window. On the 5th November, while bells were rung to commemorate '*deliverance from Guido Fawkes' plot*' of 1605, extremists destroyed the glass in the aisles and that evening a rabble shattered what remained of the east window. The rector was later seized and threatened in the church by a gang of youths. He suffered continuing harassment – once thrown into the grave at a burial he was conducting with the prayer book service – until in 1643 he fled to Oxford. Sadly, in the same year the wooden cross was removed from the spire and '*at a great cost and the hazard of many men's lives*' the carved wooden angels '*displayed on the wing*' high up on the roof were taken down and burned in the street. The years following the restoration were more settled. In 1749 the spire was rebuilt; in 1772 an organ not replaced until 1900 – was installed, and in 1777 a new peal of eight bells was hung – increased later to ten, twelve and finally thirteen.

This painting in the Cathedral shows the dramatic events of 1800 when the nave collapsed due to excavation in a burial vault; rebuilding was achieved in four years.

3

The Diocese and Cathedral

As the population of London grew in the 19th century, the link with London was severed; most of Essex was transferred to the Diocese of Rochester in 1845 and, with further demographic changes, to St. Albans in 1877. Finally a separate diocese (now the second largest in England in population) was created by Act of Parliament. Chelmsford parish church had by then been chosen after a vote of the parishes as the new cathedral, and the first bishop, John Watts-Ditchfield, took his seat here in 1914.

The dedication of the cathedral was extended to incorporate St. Peter and St. Cedd in 1954. During these years of population growth the outer north aisle had been added in 1873, and in 1878 the chancel roof raised and the present east window and clerestory windows installed. To provide more space for cathedral services the chancel was extended in the 1920s (the east window being taken down and replaced) and the vestries with a room above, now the song school, were built. In 1983 the interior was extensively refurbished – new work by contemporary artists being commissioned then and in the following years. The result is a sense of space and light throughout the whole cathedral and flexibility for worship, for diocesan events and for music and the arts. In 1990 the building of a new CHAPTER HOUSE (below), nearby provided for cathedral, diocesan and community activities.

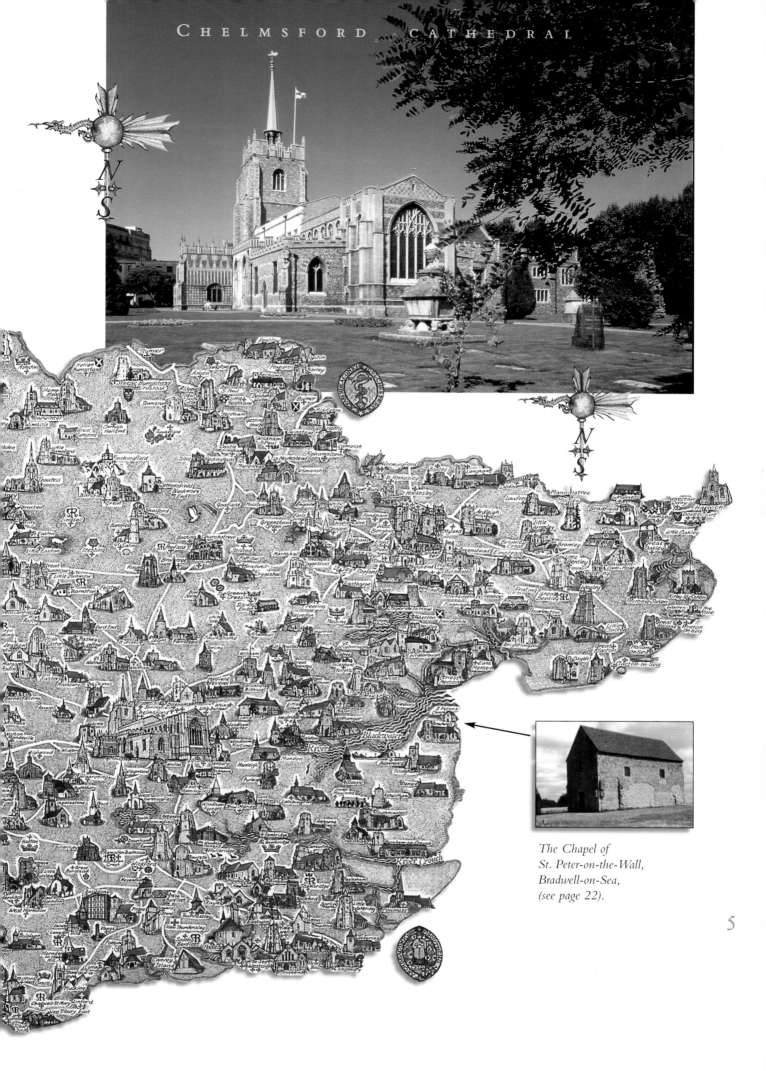

*The Chapel of
St. Peter-on-the-Wall,
Bradwell-on-Sea,
(see page 22).*

Preparing the altar for a communion service.

Grapes and a bird, details of the carving on the South Chancel door.

Plan of the Cathedral

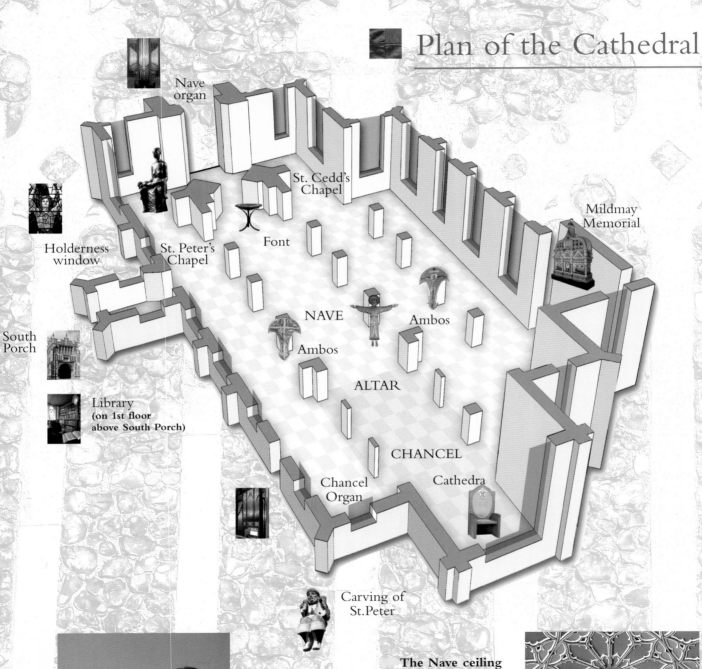

Nave organ

Holderness window

St. Peter's Chapel

St. Cedd's Chapel

Font

Mildmay Memorial

South Porch

NAVE

Ambos

Ambos

Library (on 1st floor above South Porch)

ALTAR

CHANCEL

Chancel Organ

Cathedra

Carving of St.Peter

Lighting a candle to offer a prayer.

The Nave ceiling and clerestory were the result of architect John Johnson's restoration after the collapse of 1800. The ceiling was coloured and gilded in 1961.

Tour of the interior

The Chancel

Looking east through the chancel arch, the graceful semi-circular fan arch with two sub-arches is on the left and the three-arched arcade on the right. Built in the first half of the 15th century, they separated the sanctuary from what were then two chapels built for the medieval religious guilds of Our Lady to the north and Corpus Christi to the south.

Opposite: The Chancel looking west beyond the Font to the Nave organ.

The gilding and painting of the chancel roof with its strong 'Medieval' colours were carried out in 1957 with the aid of the Friends of the Cathedral.

On the roof trusses seen from here are the arms of the Chelmsford diocese and the three other dioceses to which the church formerly belonged. Behind them (facing east) and behind the chancel arch itself are the arms of the Borough of Chelmsford, the County of Essex, the de Bourchier and de Vere families prominent in Essex in the 15th century, the Mildmay family and Westminster Abbey which possessed the manor of Moulsham until the 16th century.

8

The altar, designed by Robert Potter, architect to the 1983 re-ordering, is made of Westmorland slate weighing 1½ tons.

9

The nearby Fitzwalter memorial by James Lovell to Benjamin Mildmay, 19th Baron Fitzwalter, who died in 1756.

The two steel and bronze ambos are by contemporary sculptor, Guisseppe Lund. Above each is an ikon-style cross by Sister Petra Clare: 'Jesus of Nazareth' and 'The Cross of the Seven Doves' - representing the seven gifts of the spirit.

The original 15th century east window was described as a '*goodly fair window … in which was painted the History of Christ from his Conception to his Ascension*' and the '*Arms of the Ancient Nobility and Gentry who had contributed to the building*'. The present window was a gift in 1878 of a former rector, Archdeacon St John Mildmay, in memory of the late lady of the manor, his mother Dame Jane Mildmay. The glass in the tracery at the top depicts the Blessed Virgin Mary and eleven disciples; the eight panels depict the life and ministry of Jesus.

The COLOURFUL HANGING beneath the east window, a patchwork of 1,520 pieces, is by Beryl Dean.

The BISHOP'S CHAIR, a contemporary sculpture in stone by John Skelton, stands in front of it. On the south wall is a statue of Bishop Watts-Ditchfield. The clerestory windows, a gift of another former rector, Henry Johnson, later Bishop of Colchester, portray angels singing, playing musical instruments or bearing censers or scrolls with texts. Nearer the late 15th century chancel arch stands the Dean's stall carved in wood by John Skelton. The limestone floor here and throughout the Cathedral was laid as part of the 1983 re-ordering.

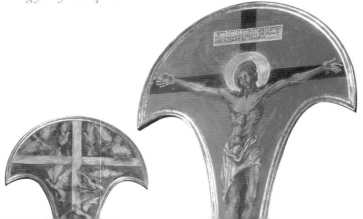

The Transepts and South Aisle

In the transept to the north of the chancel is the cathedral banner, created by Beryl Dean, presented by the Friends of the Cathedral.

To the right of the banner is the monument to Thomas Mildmay Esquire (died 1566) and his family. Thomas's father was a mercer who came to Chelmsford in 1506, acquired a market stall, and became one of the two wealthiest men in the town. Thomas Mildmay Esquire was his eldest son and advanced himself and his family in rank and wealth by becoming one of the ten 'auditors' (at a salary of £20 a year 'with profits') of the court which controlled the Crown's revenues from dissolved monastic property. From the Crown he bought first the manor of Moulsham in 1540, establishing himself as a landed gentleman, and subsequently, in 1563, the manor and advowson of Chelmsford, so that his descendants became patrons of the living for over 300 years. One of them married the heiress to the Fitzwalter title and the monument nearby (by James Lovell) is in memory of Benjamin Mildmay, 19th Baron Fitzwalter, who died in 1756. Nearby is a window depicting St. Cedd and St. Alban, the first English martyr.

Opposite: The Cathedral banner by Beryl Dean is the result of over 800 hours' work. On a background of Indian cloth of gold, the Blessed Virgin Mary is depicted in Byzantine style; the symbols are the Blessed Trinity, the Holy Spirit and the Star of Bethlehem with interlacing angels' wings. Beryl Dean's distinction in ecclesiastical embroidery extends to a considerable number of published works concerned with design and technique and the influences which bear on current developments in this field.

Below: The 16th century monument to Thomas Mildmay, his wife Avice and their family. Part of the Latin epitaph above their kneeling effigies reads in translation.

'He was a renowned esquire, she a daughter and lovely branch of William Gunson, Esq., and they had fifteen pledges of their prosperous love; seven whereof were females, eight were males'.

He and his descendants were patrons of the living for over 300 years.

The window executed in Pre-Raphaelite style by Henry Holliday, depicts the passage of the human soul along the steep path of life and through the river of death and its final joyful reception into Paradise.

WE WALK BY FAITH

MADE PERFECT IN LOVE

THE RIGHTEOUS HATH HOPE IN HIS DEATH

THE PATH WILT SHEW ME OF LIFE

THIS MORTAL MUST PUT IMMORTALITY

THE OUT OF DEPTHS HAVE I CRIED UNTO THEE

In memory of CAROLINE MAUDE HE IS able to keep that

The dearly beloved WIFE which I have committed unto HIM

of HARDWICKE HOLDERNESS 4 April 1905 against that Day

It was presented by Lieutenant Holderness in memory of his wife Catherine who died in 1905. The rich colours in this window projected by sunlight on to the limestone floor inspired Beryl Dean's designs for the kneelers bearing the names of the parishes in the diocese and worked by members of the Essex Handicrafts Association.

The doorway south of the chancel was the 'yelde door' leading from the former medieval chapel of the Corpus Christi guild to the churchyard. Close to it is a 15th century Piscina.

The window in the east wall, now largely obscured by the Chancel Organ, installed in 1995, and built by Manders, depicts two 7th century Essex saints, St. Osyth, wife of Sighere, King of the East Saxons and the reputed founder of the convent of that name in north Essex, and St. Ethelburga, abbess of Barking Abbey and sister of Earconwald who was appointed '*Bishop of London including Essex*' in 675.

On the south wall there is a curious memorial to Matthew Rudd, a churchwarden in 1590.

Two other windows here represent '*charity and mercy*' and the parable of the Good Samaritan, while two further windows in the south aisle, show biblical scenes (including the marriage in Cana and the Last Supper), and the seals of the three Essex Archdeacons. To the east, seen from here, is a gable window depicting the Holy Spirit.

The Chapels and the West End

View from St. Peter's chapel looking beyond Guisseppe Lund's bronze screen.

St. Peter's Chapel is a memorial to those who suffer in this world. The bronze sculpture *The Bombed Child* is by Georg Ehrlich, himself displaced from his native Austria following the Nazi invasion in 1938. The regimental colours hanging here include those of the local militia dating from 1808, and the west window portrays the patron saints of the armed forces. The bronze screen is by Guisseppe Lund. The etched window depicting St. Peter is by John Hutton, who engraved the great west screen in Coventry Cathedral.

The font of Westmorland slate is by Robert Potter. In the supporting pillars of the tower are two tall cupboards in which were stored banners for processions and props for the plays produced in the church and nearby in the 16th century. Records show there were parts for Christ, Aaron, Prophets, Shepherds, Vices, Devils and a '*painted Giant*', with stages for Heaven and Hell and 50 fathoms of line to manipulate '*clowds*'. The west nativity window, now obscured by the Nave Organ, installed in 1994, and built by N.P. Manders of London, replaces that destroyed in the 1939-45 war. Immediately above the wooden ceiling is the bell chamber.

'The Bombed Child' in St. Peter's Chapel, sculptured in bronze by Georg Ehrlich.

15

Within St. Cedd's chapel, which is used for daily worship and private prayer, is a figure Christus by a local sculptor Thomas Huxley Jones.

On the north wall outside the screen is a relief *Christ the Healer* by Georg Ehrlich. On the pillar to the south, brass plates which once marked '*some stone in the floor displaced*' commemorate Thomas Williamson '*whose wisdom, zeal, faith and sincerity commended are all to posterity*'. He bequeathed money in 1614 to pay for the monthly sermons which brought Thomas Hooker to the town as '*lecturer*' in 1625. Hooker was an eloquent preacher in the puritan tradition with a gift for dressing his discourse with analogies from his hearers' common experience. His position became precarious when William Laud was consecrated Bishop of London in 1628. Laud, a confidant of Charles I, and a reforming high church cleric who distrusted the influence of independent lecturers locally chosen, was determined to silence Hooker despite his strong support from the people and many of the clergy in Essex. Bound over in the sum of £50 to appear before the Court of High Commission, Hooker was persuaded to forfeit his bail and flee to Holland whence he emigrated to Massachusetts and thence to Connecticut. He is commemorated there as a '*leader of the founders of this Commonwealth*' and honoured by a statue in Hartford bearing his words from a 1638 sermon, '*The foundation of authority is laid firstly in the free consent of the people*'.

Mother and Child Bas relief in St. Cedd's Chapel by Peter Ball.

The bronze plaque 'Christ the Healer' by Georg Ehrlich.

The Nave, South Porch and Exterior

The 15th century nave was rebuilt by John Johnson after the disastrous collapse in 1800 with the arcading in its original style and with galleries which were later removed. The clerestory was lowered. For some of the pillars the original stone was re-used (on one may be seen an inverted drawing which dates from before the collapse), but for others he used Coade's artificial stone manufactured between 1770 and 1840 in Lambeth and used extensively at that time - for example on St. George's Chapel, Windsor and, nearer to home, for the ornamental features on the façade of the Shire Hall in Chelmsford. At the east end of the nave are two clerestory windows depicting scenes and texts from the Benedicite and other psalms.

Left: Outside, the walls are of flint rubble intermixed with blocks of stone. The two storeyed south porch, dating from the late 15th century, is faced with stone and flint inlay.

Access to the upper storey was probably through an aperture inside the church reached by a ladder. In 1583 it was adapted to store the parish armour - 28 corselets and headpieces being hung there. By 1718 it was being used to store the county records which were '*in utmost confusion*' damaged by wet. A few years later it was taken over by the registrar of the ecclesiastical courts, when an external brick staircase was built on. Castigated by the cathedral architect Frederic Chancellor in 1863 as an '*abominably hideous projection*', it was later removed. The room is now reached by internal stone stairs and houses a library presented to the church by the wish of Dr. John Knightbridge who died in 1677 and was the grandson of a Chelmsford tailor and churchwarden. Access to the library with its collection of theological and other works may be gained by applying to the vergers.

The Tree of Life

The artist Mark Cazalet and I met in the Cathedral and stood in front of the large north transept window. It had been blanked out when the vestry block was built beyond it, although its tracery had been left intact. The Cathedral organ used to stand here. Only after it was removed was the window revealed.

We quickly agreed that a Tree of Life would be a suitable theme for the window. Mark went away to think about it, returning some months later with a cartoon. The finished work is substantially based on that original design. It is approximately twenty feet high and consists of thirty-five wooden panels, painted in oils and fitted into the existing tracery. It portrays a huge Essex oak in high summer in full bloom although it is dying on the left-hand side ("as they all are" – an expert said to me).

The Tree of Life, of course, is there at the beginning of the Bible in the Garden of Eden (Genesis 2:9) and at the end of the Bible (Revelations 22:2), and crucially it is an image of the life giving cross of Christ.

The tree also speaks to people of every faith and none as a symbol of the challenge to our environment. On the right of the tree is an idyllic English landscape representing Thomas Traherne's vision "The corn was orient and immortal wheat." On the left of the tree there is a landfill site, with dustbin bags being bundled in. The painting asks how we can live in our environment in ways which are sustainable and do not destroy the fragile nature upon which we depend. The painting is full of details. There are a number of figures. Adam and Eve as children, run out of the wheat field, (A & E on their T-shirts). Their graffiti is on the middle of the tree trunk. St Cedd sits under the tree on the right and streams of pilgrims come

towards him. Judas Iscariot hangs from a branch on the left and from his bag thirty pieces of silver fall to the ground. This challenges us to consider whether we have sold our environment for money. Judas is portrayed a second time sitting high up in the tree on the right hand side. He is redeemed and striving upwards - see his No. 12 T-shirt. On the branch to his right are his sandwiches and thermos of coffee. There is a Purple Emperor butterfly (now extinct in Essex) – the only butterfly to eat meat, near the hanging body of Judas, and further up a Black Arches moth. You will find six birds in the painting: a great tit, a song thrush, a turtledove, a waxwing, a jay (with an acorn in its mouth), and a greater spotted woodpecker.

Mark Cazalet has produced a majestic painting, which is arresting, challenging and ecstatic.

The Organs of Chelmsford Cathedral

Specifications and background information

In 1983, Chelmsford Cathedral was closed for a scheme of complete re-ordering and refurbishment. The Victorian furnishings were removed and a splendid new limestone floor was installed with underfloor heating. Chairs replaced impossible pews and the whole building gained an enormous sense of space and dignity, as well as a vastly increased flexibility.

At the time of the re-ordering, many people remained convinced that the old Hill, Norman & Beard organ buried in its north transept position would continue to be viable for the foreseeable future. This organ had originally been built by Norman & Beard in 1898 to replace an instrument which had started life in 1772, made by Crang and Hancock and built under the western tower. Work was undertaken by Hugh Russell following the collapse of the nave roof, and the great William Hill came on the scene in 1864 when he added a swell organ and, ten years later, moved the instrument from the west end to the east end of the north aisle.

When the Cathedral authorities were encouraged to face up to the reality of the problems associated with a large organ in a very buried position, with increasingly unreliable electro-pneumatic action, there seemed to be only one possible solution: a new instrument in a new position, beneath the west tower. The decision to have an English organ with its ancestry firmly based in the work of some of the nineteenth century masters was made early in the debate, and in the light of the acoustic conditions which had been created following the re-flooring of the building.

In 1994, less than two years after launching a major appeal for the necessary funds, the Nave Organ was installed. This instrument was the first new organ to be built in an English Anglican Cathedral for more than thirty years, and the first entirely new instrument incorporating mechanical action and new casework for more than a century. The organ has four manuals and pedals, and forty stops. It has more than 2,600 pipes, the smallest of which is about ¾", and the longest being 16'. Most of the pipes are made of an alloy of tin and lead, the front display pipes being of 75% tin. Others are made of clear Quebec pine.

The organ was made entirely by hand. Each pipe is different from every other one, and the carving is also made by hand. The organ has mechanical or tracker action, which means that the keys are connected directly to the pallets or valves underneath the pipes by thin wooden trackers without making use of electrical connections. This ancient form of construction has proved to be much longer lasting than any more modern inventions, and organists prefer the direct contact with the pallets as it enables them to play more sensitively and accurately. There is over 1km of trackers in the organ, and it is expected that the instrument will last many centuries.

The Nave Organ stands firmly in the English tradition of organ-building. N.P. Mander Ltd, the organ builders, have made a particular study of the work of the great Victorian organ builders of this country, aiming at an increased understanding of how they achieved their success. This has had a consequent influence upon the style of many of their most recent organs.

They have been encouraged in their work by the growing feeling in this country that English organ-builders should be developing a native style, evolved from earlier English instruments, rather than endeavouring to copy imported concepts of questionable relevance.

The tonal scheme is clearly English, inspired by the early work of Hill, and Gray & Davison, but informed by the greater present-day understanding of the need for complete and balanced choruses. The polished oak case is inspired by the work of Dr Arthur Hill, famous for the cases at Chichester and Peterborough Cathedrals. The elegant proportions of Hill's cases stem from his application of simple geometrical principles – a practice drawn from his extensive and learned study of organ cases of the Middle Ages and Renaissance.

From the liturgical point of view, the western position of the Nave Organ posed no initial problems. Early discussions centred on moving the Cathedral Choir from its chancel position to new stalls at the west end of the nave, and of having the nave seating arranged in collegiate style. Since the major appeal to fund the building of the organ was associated with the endowment of the Choral Foundation, two fundamental features of the Cathedral's worshipping life – the Choir and the Organ – are inextricably linked. With the Choir now singing on six days each week, the thinking gradually began to move away from using a west end position for the stalls. This very exposed position, fairly close to the three principal entrances to the Cathedral, seemed less than ideal for weekday choral services when congregations tend to come and go during the course of services. For this reason, and for various others, it was decided that the Choir should, in fact, remain in the chancel stalls. The decision to keep the Choir in the chancel forced what was initially a rather unwelcome decision: the Cathedral would need to build another organ! Fortunately, the Cathedral was able to acquire pipework from the Holdich/Hill organ of 1844 which was originally installed in the church of St Andrew the Great in Cambridge, and this formed the basis of the Chancel instrument. The Chancel case, like its larger sister in the Nave, traces its ancestry to some of the fine cases of the 19th century. The overall design, executed by Donald Smith, is inspired by the coloured Dykes Bower ceiling of the chancel. Gilded and coloured carved pipe shades and brattishing are complemented by a colourful scheme for the chancel front of the instrument. Although both organs have their own independent integrity, it is possible to play all but the Choir division of the Nave Organ from the Chancel console.

The Mildmay Altar Frontal

The new altar frontal in the Mildmay Chapel to the left of the Chancel was designed and woven by Philip Sanderson of West Dean College, Chichester. It was woven in wool at their tapestry studio on a loom, which hasn't changed much since medieval times. It took 1000 hours to weave. The theme behind the design is St Cedd, who was one of four brothers who were educated on Holy Island. Two became Bishops – Chad, who founded Lichfield Cathedral, and Cedd who came to the East Saxons. He founded his Chapel at Bradwell in 654. He built it on the site of a ruined Roman fort – re-using their bricks. The Chapel survived for centuries as a haybarn, but was reconsecrated as a Church in 1920. It is now a much-loved place of pilgrimage. The frontal features both the Bradwell Chapel and various aspects of the distinctive coastline taken from photographs which Philip Sanderson took at Bradwell. The frontal also reflects the theme of pilgrimage using a series of dots and names to trace the journey from Lindisfarne to Bradwell including Lastingham in Yorkshire where Cedd had a monastery and where he died of plague (hence the drop of blood). The sweeping horizons and the vast extent of sky are caught in this tapestry. The design is very serene and still and invites the onlooker to pause and contemplate. The longer you linger the more the beauty of this tapestry will speak to you.

The Library

19

The south porch itself was greatly enriched in 1953 as a memorial to '*tasks and friendships shared*' when U.S. forces were stationed in Essex between 1942 and 1945. George Washington, whose arms are displayed here, was the great-great-grandson of an Essex rector.

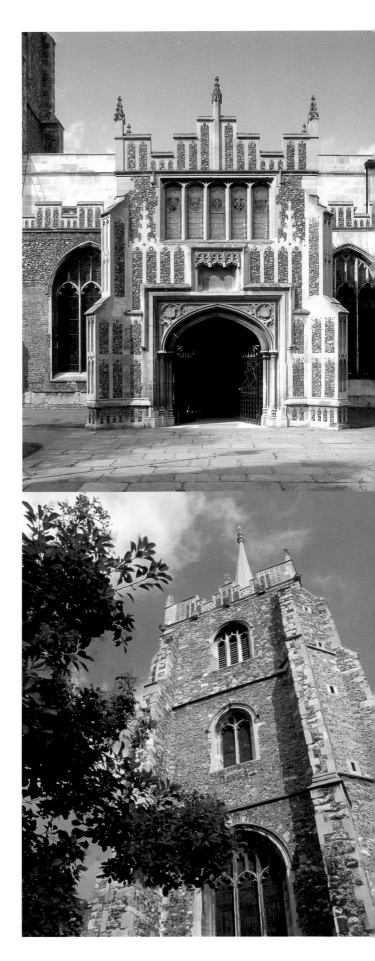

George Washington ~ the first President of the United States of America, whose great-great-grandfather was an Essex rector.

By courtesy of Sulgrave Manor

The 29 metre-high west tower is of three stages, marked outside with string courses. An inscription commemorating the rebuilding of the spire in 1749 is preserved on the tower support within St. Cedd's Chapel. The weather vane, contemporary with the rebuilt spire, is of copper, 2 metres long, portraying a dragon with its tail tucked in.

On the west door are the arms of the de Vere and de Bourchier families. At the foot of the battlements are 16 stone carvings representing the history and concerns of Essex, Chelmsford, and the church. They are by Huxley Jones, as is also the carving of St. Peter on the south-east corner of the south transept.

Over the years the best that artist and craftsman can supply has been employed; the future will see further change, some perhaps in the lifetime of this guide, aimed always at the cathedral's first responsibility - to lead people to worship and prayer and to the knowledge and the love of God.

Chapel of St. Peter-on-the-Wall

Bradwell-on-sea ~
a place of pilgrimage

Bradwell is a quiet, secluded village, on the southern bank of the estuary of the Blackwater, where it joins the sea. Most villages are remarkable for the two kinds of building: parish church, and manor house or castle. Bradwell not only has both church and houses of interest, but this ancient Saxon chapel of St. Peter-on-the-Wall, built by St. Cedd on the western wall of the former Roman military station of Othona.

This isolated chapel of St. Peter-on-the-Wall, has stood as a place of Christian worship for over 1,300 years.

Each year on the first Saturday in July, Christians make an annual pilgrimage to this place, the deepest living root of the church in this country. St. Cedd, who built this chapel in the A.D. 654, was invited by King Sigbert to bring the good news of Jesus to the East Saxons. The Chapel still stands to this day as a witness to the same message, as relevant to our lives today as ever before.

A Summer Evening Service.

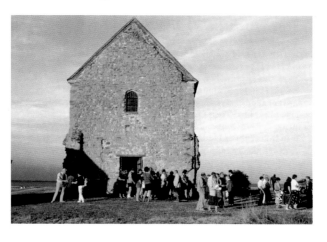

The Chapel Altar

The Chapel Altar was consecrated at the Bradwell Pilgrimage, on the 6th July 1985 by the Bishop of Chelmsford and the Bishop of Brentwood. The three stones set in the supporting pillar represent the three other communities involved in St. Cedd's ministry:

The left stone is a gift from Holy Island, Lindisfarne, Northumberland. St. Cedd was trained there by St. Aidan, apostle of the North and came to preach the Gospel to the East Saxons at the request of King Sigbert.

The centre stone is a gift from the Island of Iona where the Celtic mission in Britain began. St. Columba founded a monastery where the missionary monks were trained, and included St. Aidan who was later sent to Lindisfarne.

The right stone is a gift from Lastingham. Bishop Cedd left Bradwell to build a monastery at Lastingham, in the Yorkshire Moors, where he died of the plague at Lastingham in October 664 A.D.

23

The church is perhaps the oldest church in England of which so much remains - and partly as the sole monument of the short-lived Anglo-Celtic Church of the East Saxons.

In A.D. 405, five years before the fall of Rome, St. Patrick carried the Gospels to Ireland. During two centuries of anarchy and confusion on the continent, the Celtic Church developed in a hard school of poverty and adventure, cut off from the mingled politics and theology of the Mediterranean world. In 563 St. Columba crossed to Scotland, where Christianity had earlier penetrated beyond the Wall and was still remembered. He settled on Iona, and in 635 Aidan, one of the monks of his foundation, crossed the country to Northumbria and there founded the island monastery of Lindisfarne. The Celts had been reproached by Bede for their failure to evangelise the Saxon invaders. Had history allowed them to reply, they might have remarked on the Saxon reluctance to learn from a people they despised and had defeated, and it was perhaps to avoid this difficulty that Aidan trained twelve young Englishmen as missionaries. One of these was Cedd, and after considerable success in the Midlands he was sent south in answer to an appeal from King Sigbert. In 653 he landed, on the quay of the old Roman fort of Othona, and travelled the kingdom of the East Saxons. After returning to the north for consecration as bishop, he came south again and built churches here, at Tilbury, probably at Prittlewell, perhaps at Mersea, and at other places whose names are now lost.

In 664, when the key differences between the Roman and Celtic churches (in particular the dating of Easter) were debated at the Synod of Whitby, Cedd, who acted as interpreter, adhered to Canterbury and to Rome, and the authority of the Celtic Church retreated northward. Much of its outlook and practice, however, remained, and the spirit of the Celtic church, its integrity, its mysticism, and its love of nature, has contributed a strand to the complex pattern of English life ever since. It may be thought that those who use the bird watchers' cottage near-by are perpetuating the Celtic heritage as well as those who use the chapel.

St. Cedd's principal foundation was a community, at once missionary and monastic, here at St. Peter's, which may be considered the first cathedral of Essex. He made another, a monastery at Lastingham, in a valley of the Yorkshire moors. His wooden church there was soon rebuilt but still shows some Saxon work. St. Cedd died of plague at Lastingham in October 664, and when his people at Bradwell learnt that he would visit them no more, thirty of them journeyed up the coast, and all but one, a boy, shared his end. Soon after, Essex was taken into the diocese of London, and St. Peter's became a minster, the chief church for the surrounding country. Southminster was probably so named in relation to it.

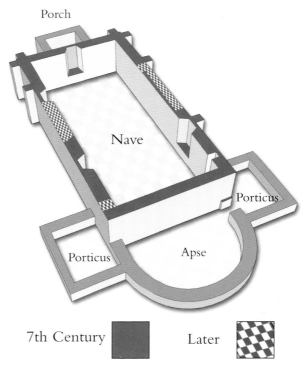

Porch

Nave

Porticus

Porticus

Apse

7th Century

Later

Probable reconstruction